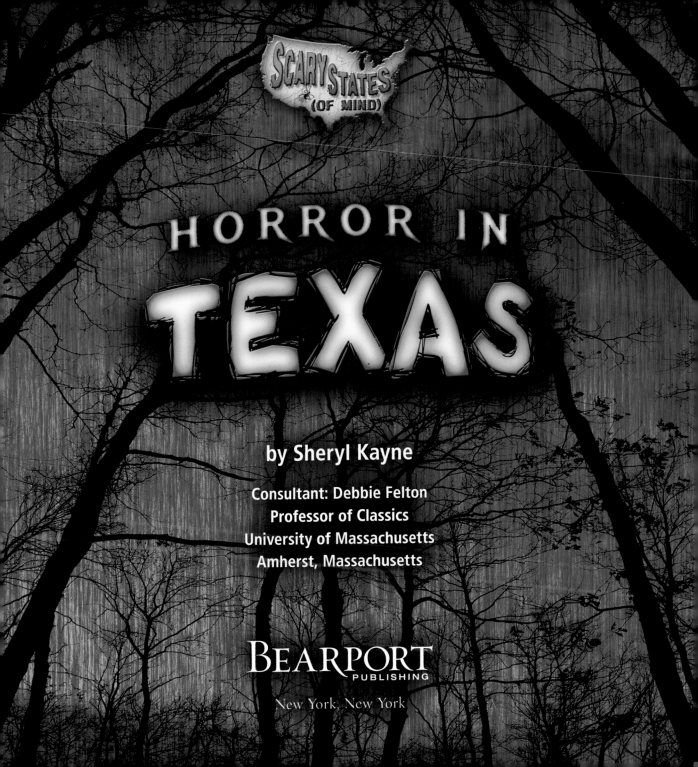

SCARY STATES
(OF MIND)

HORROR IN
TEXAS

by Sheryl Kayne

Consultant: Debbie Felton
Professor of Classics
University of Massachusetts
Amherst, Massachusetts

BEARPORT
PUBLISHING

New York, New York

Credits

Cover, © Chris Hinkley/Shutterstock and © Teri James/Shutterstock; TOC, © James Laurie/Shutterstock; 4–5, © photofriday/Shutterstock, © xradiophotog/Shutterstock, and © vovan/Shutterstock; 6–7, © Giulian Garruba/Shutterstock; 6R, © South_agency/iStock; 8, © photomaster/Shutterstock; 9, © GlebSStock/Shutterstock; 10, © falun/iStock; 11, © Sjo/iStock; 12L, © Google Data Maps 2019; 12R, © ju_see/Shutterstock; 13, © MTFCA; 14T, © Artsiom Petrushenka/Shutterstock; 14B, © Anucha Tiemsom/Shutterstock and © luis abrantes/Shutterstock; 15T, © CWT Texans/CC BY-SA 4.0; 15B, © Our Haunted Vacations; 16, © Khomenko Maryna/Shutterstock; 17, © Kondor83/Shutterstock and © 21MARCH/Shutterstock; 18–19, © Thomas Hawk/CC BY-NC 4.0; 20, © Joe Belanger/Shutterstock; 20–21, © kawing921/Shutterstock and © Rawpixel.com/Shutterstock; 23, © Charles Harker/Shutterstock; 24, © IrinaK/Shutterstock.

Publisher: Kenn Goin
Senior Editor: Joyce Tavolacci
Creative Director: Spencer Brinker
Photo Researcher: Thomas Persano
Cover: Kim Jones

Library of Congress Cataloging-in-Publication Data

Names: Kayne, Sheryl Wolff, author.
Title: Horror in Texas / by Sheryl Kayne.
Description: New York: Bearport Publishing Company, Inc., 2020. | Series: Scary states (of mind) | Includes bibliographical references and index.
Identifiers: LCCN 2019014400 (print) | LCCN 2019017821 (ebook) | ISBN 9781642805673 (ebook) | ISBN 9781642805130 (library)
Subjects: LCSH: Haunted places—Texas—Juvenile literature. | Ghosts—Texas—Juvenile literature. | Texas—Miscellanea—Juvenile literature.
Classification: LCC BF1472.U6 (ebook) | LCC BF1472.U6 K39 2020 (print) | DDC 133.109764—dc23
LC record available at https://lccn.loc.gov/2019014400

For more information, write to Bearport Publishing Company, Inc., 45 West 21st Street, Suite 3B, New York, New York 10010. Printed in the United States of America.

10 9 8 7 6 5 4 3 2 1

CONTENTS

HORROR IN TEXAS

By day, everything is big and bright in Texas. However, when night falls, there's another side to the Lone Star State. Ghosts wander along empty roads. **Spirits** haunt hotels. And spooky figures hide in shadows.

Get ready to read four
terrifying stories about Texas.
Turn the page . . . if you dare.

THE WET GHOST

White Rock Lake, Dallas

White Rock Lake is known for boating and fishing. It's also famous for a spooky, soaked spirit.

It was a moonlit night in the 1950s. A couple was driving around the lake. Their headlights lit up something strange. A young blonde woman in a long wet dress was walking barefoot down the road. She asked the couple for a ride to Gaston Avenue. They agreed, and she got into the back seat.

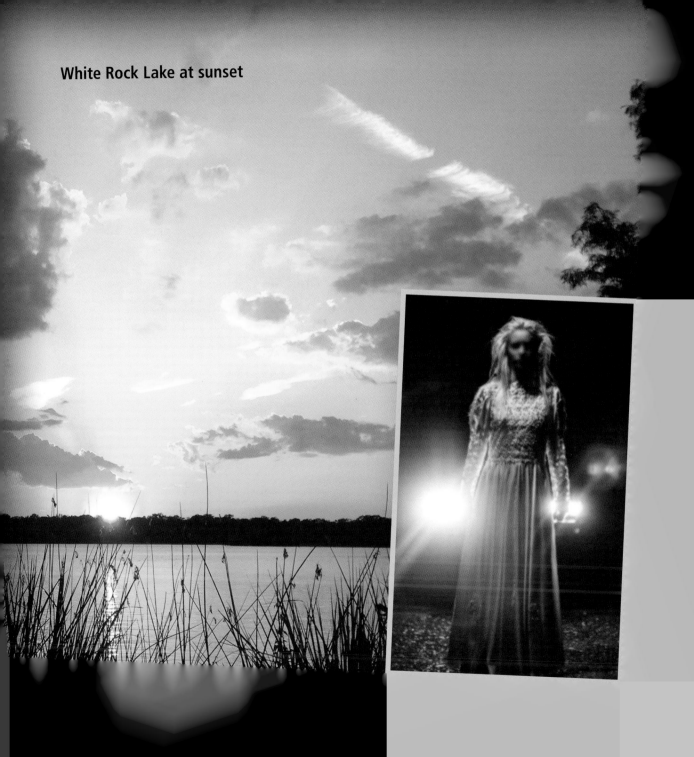

White Rock Lake at sunset

As the car pulled forward, the woman stared out the window. Her wet hair blew in the night breeze. When their car arrived at Gaston Avenue, the couple found that the back seat was empty. The woman was gone! All that was left in her place was a puddle of water.

According to **legend**, a young woman died in a boating accident on White Rock Lake. When there's a full moon, her ghost appears, asking for a ride.

TERROR ON THE TRACKS

Train Track Crossing, New Braunfels

On March 28, 1920, the Smith family piled into their Model T car. They were off to see family in nearby Seguin. Sadly, they never arrived. As their car crossed a railroad track, the family heard a rumbling sound. Before they knew it, a train had slammed into their car.

A Ford Model T

The train dragged the Smith family's car down the tracks. The Model T was ripped to shreds. A mother, her three daughters, and a granddaughter, Katherine, were all killed.

The Smiths were later buried. However, one **grave** held two people. Three-year-old Katherine was buried in her mother's arms—linked forever.

Today, drivers have experienced an uneasy feeling at the accident site. Are the spirits of the Smith family trapped there?

A crushed Model T
after an accident

13

SPOOKY SLEEPOVER

The Jefferson Hotel, Jefferson

The **historic** Jefferson Hotel is said to be one of Texas's most haunted places. Guests have a choice of spooky rooms. Room 19 is a favorite. Some people believe that a woman hanged herself there over 100 years ago.

"I know there are things that are unexplainable that happen in the hotel," said one of the Jefferson's managers.

The Jefferson Hotel dates to 1851.

Inside the hotel

One night, **ghost hunters** stayed in room 19. They brought a special tool to detect ghosts. They soon felt a strong **presence** in the room. They asked it: "Are you a female?" The tool **indicated** that the ghost answered "Yes!"

Room 17 is also said to be haunted. One night, a guest heard spooky voices while his wife slept soundly next to him. When they showered in the morning, a message appeared on the steamy bathroom mirror. It read "Get out!"

In 1912, a woman took her own life in the hotel. She hanged herself after her **fiancé** did not show up for their wedding.

17

Haunted High School

El Paso High School, El Paso

In the 1980s, Danny McKillip was a track coach at El Paso High School. Late one night after a **meet,** he and his team entered the locker room. Suddenly, Coach Danny and the students heard cheering upstairs in the **auditorium.** He ran to **investigate.** His hand touched the doorknob and the sound stopped. Coach Danny peeked inside, and the room was dark and empty!

El Paso High School
opened in 1916.

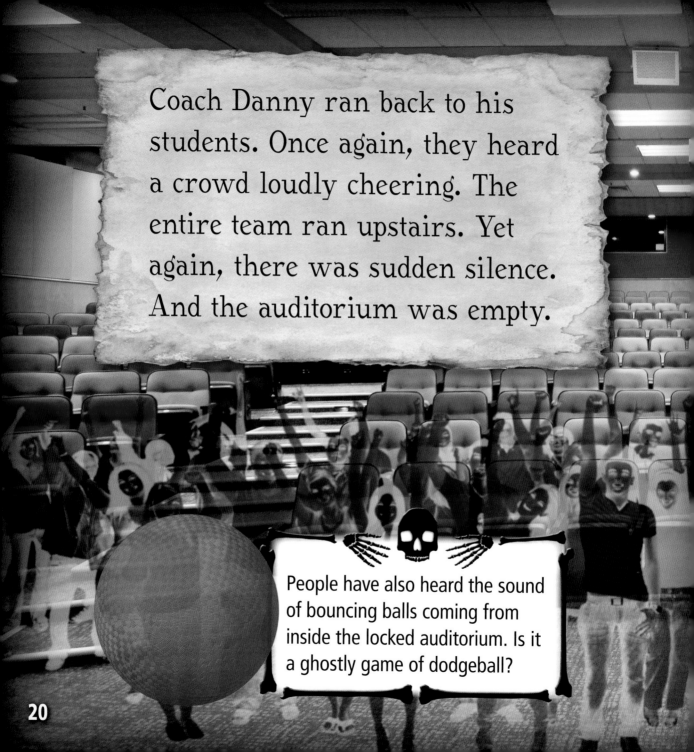

Coach Danny ran back to his students. Once again, they heard a crowd loudly cheering. The entire team ran upstairs. Yet again, there was sudden silence. And the auditorium was empty.

People have also heard the sound of bouncing balls coming from inside the locked auditorium. Is it a ghostly game of dodgeball?

Spooky Spots in Texas

White Rock Lake
A young woman haunts this lake and just wants to go home.

El Paso High School
Discover an auditorium full of cheering ghosts.

NEW MEXICO

OKLAHOMA

TEXAS

The Jefferson Hotel
Which haunted room will you stay in?

CANADA

UNITED STATES

MEXICO

Train Track Crossing, New Braunfels
Visit the scene of a horrific train accident.

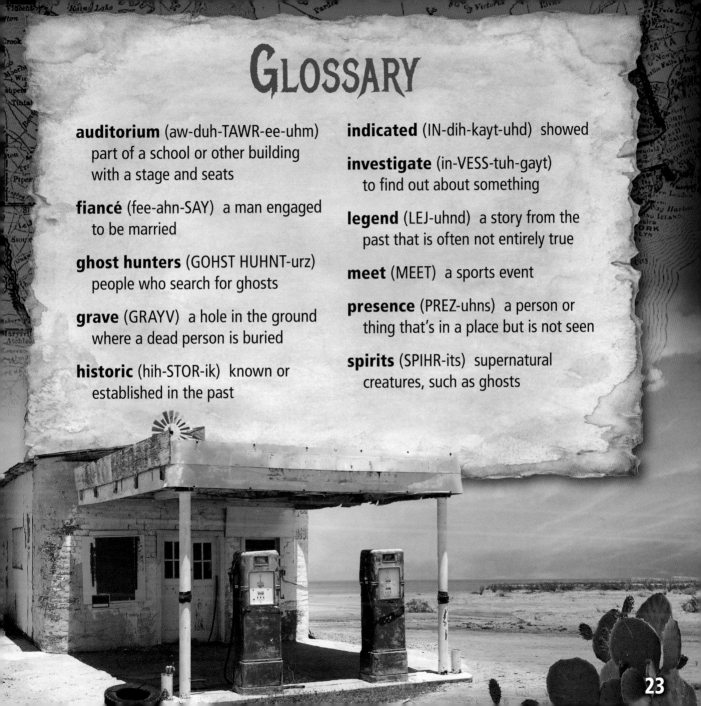

Glossary

auditorium (aw-duh-TAWR-ee-uhm) part of a school or other building with a stage and seats

fiancé (fee-ahn-SAY) a man engaged to be married

ghost hunters (GOHST HUHNT-urz) people who search for ghosts

grave (GRAYV) a hole in the ground where a dead person is buried

historic (hih-STOR-ik) known or established in the past

indicated (IN-dih-kayt-uhd) showed

investigate (in-VESS-tuh-gayt) to find out about something

legend (LEJ-uhnd) a story from the past that is often not entirely true

meet (MEET) a sports event

presence (PREZ-uhns) a person or thing that's in a place but is not seen

spirits (SPIHR-its) supernatural creatures, such as ghosts

Index

Read More

Camisa, Kathryn. *Creepy Schools (Tiptoe Into Scary Places).* New York: Bearport (2018).

Markovics, Joyce. *Chilling Cemeteries (Tiptoe Into Scary Places).* New York: Bearport (2017).

Learn More Online

To learn more about the horror in Texas, visit:

www.bearportpublishing.com/ScaryStates

About the Author

Sheryl Kayne is a writer who also teaches writing. She loves researching, writing, and telling stories. In her free time, she likes to read, talk, and write.